simple starters

simple starters

easy recipes for effortless entertaining

RYLAND
PETERS
& SMALL
LONDON NEW YORK

Recipe credits

Valerie Aikman-Smith
Gazpacho with smoked salted
  toasts
Parmesan wafers
Pretzel bites
Salt-crusted citrus prawns with
  chilli dipping sauce

Fiona Beckett
Cheese and basil soufflés
French onion soup
Pea and Parma ham crostini
Seared steak carpaccio with
  truffle vinaigrette and rocket

Maxine Clark
Cherry tomato, bocconcini and
  basil salad on bruschetta
Parma ham with figs and
  balsamic dressing
Spicy crab in filo cups

Ross Dobson
Chickpea, tomato and green bean
  minestrone
Chilli salt squid
Naked ravioli with sage cream

Lydia France
Grilled lamb skewers with garlic
  and saffron custard
Prawn cocktail shots
Vermouth scallops with green
  olive tapenade

Tonia George
Crab bisque
Pea and smoked ham soup
  with mint

Louise Pickford
Fresh asparagus with hollandaise
  sauce

Jennie Shapter
Mini spring rolls with chilli
  dipping sauce

Fiona Smith
Chicken liver pâté with blueberry
  and balsamic glaze
Classic Caesar salad
Double courgette and Parmesan
  salad
Pickled salmon with fennel and
  cucumber
Pork and hazelnut rillettes with
  pickled cucumbers
Smoked mackerel and preserved
  lemon pâté
Smoked mushroom pâté

Laura Washburn
Apple, beetroot and fennel salad
  with Roquefort

Photography Credits

Martin Brigdale
Pages 21, 40, 44
Peter Cassidy
Pages 4–5, 9, 34, 43,
47, 51, 56
Jean Cazals
pages 14, 17, 18
Lisa Cohen
page 6
Gus Filgate
endpapers, pages 2, 39
Jonathan Gregson
pages 13, 26, 29, 48
Richard Jung
pages 1, 25, 29, 59
William Lingwood
page 10
Diana Miller
pages 33, 37, 52
Yuki Sugiura
pages 22, 30
Ian Wallace
page 63
Kate Whitaker
pages 55, 60
Polly Wreford
page 3

Commissioning Editor Julia Charles
Production Controller Toby Marshall
Picture Researcher Emily Westlake
Art Director Leslie Harrington
Publishing Director Alison Starling

Indexer Hilary Bird

First published in the
United Kingdom in 2010
by Ryland Peters & Small
20–21 Jockey's Fields
London WC1R 4BW
www.rylandpeters.com

Text © Valerie Aikman-Smith,
Fiona Beckett, Maxine Clark,
Ross Dobson, Lydia France,
Tonia George, Louise Pickford,
Jennie Shapter, Fiona Smith,
Laura Washburn and Ryland
Peters & Small 2010
Design and photographs
© Ryland Peters & Small 2010

ISBN: 978 1 84597 997 3

10 9 8 7 6 5 4 3 2 1

A CIP record for this book is available
from the British Library.

Printed in China

Notes
• All spoon measurements are level unless
otherwise specified.
• Eggs used in the recipes in this book are
medium unless specified otherwise.
• Ovens should be preheated to the specified
temperatures. All ovens work slightly differently.
We recommend using an oven thermometer
and suggest you consult the maker's handbook
for any special instructions, particularly if you
are cooking in a fan-assisted oven, as you will
need to adjust temperatures according to
manufacturer's instructions.

contents

the best start

When entertaining at home, whether you are hosting an informal supper party or planning an impressive dinner for a special occasion, you'll want your meal to get off to the best start.

The first course you choose to serve is all important as it whets the appetite and hints at what is to follow. Here, in *Simple Starters*, you will find a perfect selection of easy-to-prepare yet delicious recipes for both small bites to serve with drinks and plated starters. Using only the freshest of ingredients, many of the recipes have an international influence but some are more familiar favourites.

The book features a variety of dishes taken from the colourful cuisines of the Mediterranean, inspired by the exotic flavours of Morocco and the Middle East, or spiced up with exciting South East Asian ingredients. What unites all the recipes is that they are surprisingly quick and easy to prepare and guaranteed to impress your guests.

To take the stress out of entertaining, many of the dishes can also be made well ahead of time and simply finished off or reheated as necessary once you are ready to serve. What's more, you will find that some of the recipes can be adapted to make more substantial dishes that can be enjoyed for lunch or as a light supper.

In *Simple Starters* you'll find plenty of inspiration and something to suit all tastes and every style of occasion, enabling you to enjoy stress-free entertaining time and time again.

small bites

pea and parma ham crostini

250 g fresh or frozen peas

2 spring onions

40 g finely grated Parmesan

1 tablespoon finely chopped fresh mint or dill

2 tablespoons fruity olive oil

freshly squeezed lemon juice, to taste

sea salt and freshly ground black pepper

125 g thinly sliced Parma ham or other air dried ham, torn or cut into strips

CIABATTA TOASTS

2 ready-to-bake ciabatta loaves

olive oil spray or 4–6 tablespoons light olive oil

MAKES 18 CROSTINI

New season peas are deliciously sweet and make a perfect topping for crispy crostini. Salty Parma ham creates a lovely contrast in flavour but for a meat-free version simply omit the ham and top with generous shavings of Parmesan.

Preheat the oven to 180°C (350°F) Gas 4. Cut the ciabatta on the slant into fairly thin slices. Spray both sides with olive oil or pour the olive oil onto a baking tray and dip the slices of ciabatta into it. Bake in the preheated oven for 15 minutes, turning the slices halfway through the cooking time. Repeat with any remaining ciabatta slices. Let cool. (These toasts can be made in advance and stored in an airtight container until you are ready to top them.)

Cook the peas in plenty of lighly salted boiling water for 2–3 minutes, until just tender. Drain under cold running water. Trim and cut the spring onions in half lengthways, then slice them very thinly.

Put the peas and onions in a food processor and pulse until you get a chunky spread. Add the pecorino and mint and pulse again, then stir in the olive oil. Season to taste with salt, pepper and lemon juice. Spread the mixture thickly on the ciabatta toasts and drape a piece of ham on top. Don't wait too long before serving as the toasts will become soggy.

mini spring rolls
with chilli dipping sauce

2 tablespoons sunflower oil

50 g carrots, cut into matchsticks

50 g mangetouts, cut into matchsticks

50 g shiitake mushrooms, chopped

2.5 cm fresh ginger, peeled and grated

1 small red chilli, deseeded and chopped

50 g bean sprouts

2 spring onions, thinly sliced

1 tablespoon light soy sauce

2 teaspoons plain flour

8 x 20 cm square spring-roll wrappers

oil for deep-frying

a deep-fat fryer

CHILLI DIPPING SAUCE

5 tablespoons sweet chilli sauce

1 tablespoon light soy sauce

MAKES 16 ROLLS

Spring rolls are best served immediately after cooking, but to keep last-minute preparation minimal you can make the filling up to 24 hours ahead. Fill the spring roll wrappers about 1 hour before cooking, but keep them covered so they remain moist until cooked.

Heat the sunflower oil in a wok or frying pan and stir-fry the carrots, mangetouts, mushrooms and ginger for 1 minute. Add the chilli, bean sprouts and spring onions and stir-fry for 1–2 minutes, or until the vegetables are tender-crisp. Remove from the heat, stir in the soy sauce and set aside to cool.

Next, make the chilli dipping sauce. Mix together the sweet chilli sauce and soy sauce in a small bowl and transfer to a serving dish.

In a small bowl, mix the plain flour with 1 tablespoon water to make a paste. Cut the spring-roll wrappers in half diagonally and place under a damp cloth to keep moist. Remove one at a time to fill.

Divide the filling into four and put a quarter of one batch on the long cut side of a wrapper, placing it along the centre, slightly in from the edge. Fold over the side flaps. Brush a little flour paste on the pointed end of the wrapper and roll up towards the point, pressing the end to seal. Repeat with the remaining wrappers. Keep covered until ready to cook.

Fill a deep-fryer with oil to the manufacturer's recommended level. Heat the oil to 180°C (350°F) and deep-fry the rolls in batches for 2–3 minutes, until crisp and golden. Drain on kitchen paper. Serve with the chilli dipping sauce.

pretzel bites

250 ml warm water
2 tablespoons butter, at room temperature, cubed
3 teaspoons fast-action dried yeast
1 teaspoon white sugar
400 g plain flour
4 teaspoons baking powder
sea salt flakes, for topping
American mustard, to serve (optional)

MAKES ABOUT 40 BITES

In a glass measuring jug, mix together the warm water, butter, yeast and sugar. Stir until the butter has melted. Put the flour in a food processor. With the motor running, pour the liquid into the flour in a steady stream until all of it is incorporated and the dough forms a ball. Add a little extra flour if necessary. Put the dough on a floured work surface and knead for 2 minutes. Form into a ball and put in an oiled bowl. Cover with a tea towel and leave to prove in a warm place for 1 hour.

Preheat the oven to 220°C (425°F) Gas 7. Turn the dough out onto a floured work surface and roll into a 30 x 15 cm rectangle. Cut 2.5 cm strips of dough from the long side and cut these into 2.5 cm bite-sized pieces.

Put 1 litre water in a non-stick wok or pan (do not use aluminium), add the baking powder and bring to the boil. Drop the dough pieces into the water for about 1 minute and remove with a slotted spoon onto non-stick baking trays. They will puff up. Sprinkle with salt flakes and bake in the preheated oven for 10–15 minutes until brown on top. Serve with American mustard for dipping.

parmesan and sage wafers

These delicate lacy wafers are ideal with a glass of prosecco, or try them instead of croûtons on a Caesar salad (see page 34).

110 g Parmesan, grated
1 tablespoon finely chopped fresh sage
coarsely ground black pepper
sea salt flakes, for topping

MAKES 14 WAFERS

Preheat the oven to 180°C (350°F) Gas 4.

Mix together the Parmesan and sage and season with black pepper.

Drop tablespoons of the mixture at 5 cm intervals on a non-stick baking tray. Pat down the mounds with your fingers. Bake in the preheated oven for 5–6 minutes until the mixture is completely melted and the edges are turning golden brown. Keep an eye on them as they brown fast.

Remove the wafers from the oven and set aside for a few moments to firm up. They will be soft when they come out of the oven but will harden as they cool.

With a spatula, carefully remove the wafers and arrange them on a wire rack to cool completely. Once cooled, sprinkle with salt flakes. They can be stored in an airtight container for 2 days.

grilled lamb skewers
with garlic and saffron custard

500 g lamb loin fillet, cut into 30 cubes

2 tablespoons olive oil

1 tablespoon finely chopped fresh oregano

freshly ground black pepper

GARLIC AND SAFFRON CUSTARD

50 g butter

8–10 garlic cloves, coarsely grated

½ teaspoon saffron strands

500 ml double cream

grated zest and freshly squeezed juice of 1 small lemon

sea salt, to taste

30 small wooden skewers, each about 15 cm long, soaked in water for 30 minutes before use

MAKES 30

The wonderful garlic and saffron sauce has the consistency of custard, but doesn't actually contain eggs. If it becomes too thick, you can dilute with a little lemon juice or white wine. It makes the perfect accompaniment to the skewers.

Put the olive oil, oregano and black pepper in a dish. Add the lamb cubes, cover and marinate for about 2 hours.

When you are ready to cook, preheat the grill to medium.

Thread the lamb cubes onto the prepared wooden skewers and put them on a baking tray, loosely covering the exposed parts of the sticks with a little foil to prevent them from scorching. Set aside.

To make the custard, gently heat the butter, garlic and saffron together in a large, heavy-based frying pan. Add half the double cream and simmer until the cream bubbles and thickens, then add the lemon juice and turn down the heat.

Grill the lamb skewers under the preheated grill for 2–3 minutes on each side and keep warm until ready to serve.

Add the remaining cream, lemon zest and a little salt to the saffron cream mixture and stir over low heat until you have a custard-like sauce. Pour into a bowl and serve warm with the lamb skewers.

prawn cocktail shots

200 g crème fraîche or
soured cream

2 tablespoons tomato ketchup

2 teaspoons Manzanilla sherry

15 g each fresh tarragon leaves
and fresh dill, chopped

1 teaspoon Spanish smoked
paprika (pimentòn)

a pinch of celery salt

15 g spring onions, roughly
chopped

400–500 g cooked and peeled
king prawns (about 60), tails
left on

1 tablespoon snipped fresh
chives or a pinch of Spanish
smoked paprika (pimentòn),
to garnish

freshly ground black pepper

shot glasses
cocktail sticks

MAKES 30 SHOTS

These miniature prawn cocktails are an updated version of the seventies classic. To make them eye-catching you will need small, sturdy shot glasses and good-looking cocktail sticks. If preferred, you can arrange a little finely shredded iceberg lettuce at the bottom of the glasses in place of the spring onions.

To make the cocktail sauce, put the crème fraîche, ketchup, sherry, herbs, paprika and celery salt in a small bowl. Mix with a fork or small whisk until well combined and smooth.

Spoon a little cocktail sauce into each shot glass and add a few chopped spring onions. Add 2 prawns to each shot glass and garnish with either a sprinkling of chives or a pinch of smoked paprika, as preferred. Grind over some black pepper, if liked.

Serve immediately with cocktail sticks for spearing the prawns.

vermouth scallops
with green olive tapenade

500 g fresh scallops (30–40)

1 tablespoon dry vermouth

2 tablespoons olive oil

1 cured chorizo sausage
(about 300 g)

sea salt and freshly ground
black pepper

GREEN OLIVE TAPENADE

90 g green olives, stoned

3 spring onions, finely chopped

1 large garlic clove

2 tablespoons dry vermouth

1 tablespoon chopped fresh flat
leaf parsley

½ teaspoon sea salt

a griddle pan
cocktail sticks

MAKES 30–40

This is a substantial yet elegant bite and one that lovers of a classic Martini cocktail will enjoy; it's a great way to kick off a dinner party. The scallops can also be served on thick slices of cucumber; one large cucumber is sufficient for this quantity of scallops. Try the delicious olive tapenade simply served spread on Ciabatta Toasts (see page 8).

Put the scallops in a large bowl with the 1 tablespoon dry vermouth, olive oil and a pinch each of salt and black pepper. Cover and let sit for about 10 minutes.

Heat a griddle pan over high heat until very hot and sear the scallops for 1 minute on each side. Do not move the scallops during cooking – they are very fragile and they may tear.

Put the olives, spring onions, garlic, 2 tablespoons dry vermouth and parsley in a food processor with ½ teaspoon salt and give it a few short sharp blasts until the tapenade mixture looks chopped but not too mushy. Slice the chorizo so you have a slice for each scallop (not too thinly as you want it to support the weight of the scallop).

To assemble, spoon a little tapenade onto each chorizo slice, put a seared scallop on top and secure with a cocktail stick to serve.

spicy crab in filo cups

FILO CUPS
9 sheets filo pastry
50 g butter, melted

SPICY CRAB FILLING
200 g tinned white crab meat in brine, drained
75 g tinned water chestnuts, drained and finely chopped
3 cm piece of fresh ginger, peeled and cut into fine strips
2 spring onions, trimmed and finely sliced
finely grated zest and juice of 1 lime
1 garlic clove, crushed
½ fresh red chilli, deseeded and finely chopped
2 teaspoons sesame oil
2 tablespoons chopped fresh coriander leaves
sea salt and freshly ground black pepper

3 mini muffin tins, 12 holes each, brushed with melted butter

MAKES ABOUT 36 CUPS

These delicate bites are as light as air, but packed with fresh Asian flavours. Use tinned white crab meat from the Pacific for these – not only does it taste very good, but there is no shell or messy bits to deal with if catering for a large number of people. It is also much cheaper than fresh crabmeat.

Preheat the oven to 180°C (350°F) Gas 4.

Unroll the filo. Stack the sheets on top of each other, then score the top sheet into 12 squares. Cut down through all the layers, giving 108 squares. Pile into 2–3 stacks and keep beside you in a plastic bag.

To make a filo cup, take 3 squares of filo, brush each with melted butter and lay one on top of the other, so that the points make a star, and do not touch each other. Quickly but gently press into one of the holes of the prepared muffin tin, so the points of the filo shoot upwards like a handkerchief. Repeat with all the remaining filo until you have 36 cups.

Bake in the preheated oven for about 8–10 minutes until golden. Remove, let cool in the tin, then carefully transfer to a tray.

Put the crab meat in a bowl and fluff up with a fork. Stir in the water chestnuts, ginger and spring onions. In a separate bowl, mix the lime zest and juice, crushed garlic, chilli and sesame oil, and season to taste. Mix this into the crab mixture (this can be done up to 4 hours in advance), then stir in the chopped coriander.

Fill the cups with the crab mixture just before serving (they can go a little soggy if they are kept too long).

soups

pea and smoked ham soup with mint

3 tablespoons olive oil, plus extra to serve

6 spring onions, chopped

2 garlic cloves, sliced

200 g thick slices of smoked ham, cut into cubes

1 tablespoon chopped fresh mint leaves or 1 teaspoon dried mint

500 g peas (defrosted or fresh)

1 litre hot chicken or vegetable stock

sea salt and freshly ground black pepper

SERVES 4

Frozen or fresh peas make a very satisfying sweet and savoury base for a soup. If you are into podding your own peas from the garden, the results will be even better, but frozen peas pulled out of the freezer are just as good as a standby.

Heat the olive oil in a large saucepan over low heat and add the spring onions. Cook for 2–3 minutes, then add the garlic, ham and half the mint and cook for a further 2 minutes, stirring. Stir in the peas and pour in the hot stock. Simmer for 2–3 minutes until the peas are tender.

Transfer a third of the soup to a blender and liquidize until completely smooth. Pour back into the soup and mix until amalgamated. Season with just a little sea salt (the ham will be quite salty already) and some freshly ground black pepper. Add the remaining mint.

Divide the soup between 4 bowls and serve with a drizzle of olive oil and a fresh grinding of black pepper.

French onion soup

1 sourdough baguette
or other long rustic loaf

2 tablespoons olive oil

50 g unsalted butter

2–3 large mild onions (about
700 g in total), thinly sliced

½ teaspoon sugar

½ teaspoon dried thyme

150 ml dry white wine

1.25 litres beef, chicken or
vegetable stock

white wine vinegar, to taste
(optional)

125 g Gruyère (rind removed),
coarsely grated

sea salt and freshly ground
black pepper

SERVES 4

French onion soup is one of the classic bistro dishes, made luxuriant by its melting cheese and crisp bread topping. Like many simple recipes it needs really good ingredients. The critical thing to remember is to cook the onions long enough and to use a substantial, densely textured bread, preferably a couple of days old.

Preheat the oven to 180°C (350°F) Gas 4. Cut the bread into slices about 2 cm thick and lay on a baking tray. Bake in the preheated oven for 15–20 minutes or until crisp and lightly browned, then set aside. (You can do this ahead when you have the oven on.)

Heat the oil in a large ovenproof casserole, add the butter and tip in the onions. Stir so that they're thoroughly coated with oil and cook over low/medium heat, stirring them occasionally, until they turn a rich, deep brown. This may take up to 40 minutes, depending on your onions. Add the sugar once they start to brown, and stir more regularly — you don't want to burn them. Once the onions are a good colour, stir in the thyme and wine and leave it to bubble up and reduce by half. Add the stock, bring back to the boil and simmer for about 20–25 minutes. Check the seasoning, adding salt and pepper to taste and a few drops of vinegar if you think it tastes too sweet. Preheat the grill.

Ladle the soup into 4 individual heatproof bowls. Lay the slices of bread over the surface of the soup, pressing them down lightly. Scatter over the Gruyère and grill for 5–10 minutes until the cheese is bubbling. Serve immediately.

gazpacho
with smoked salted toasts

1.3 kg tomatoes

1 garlic clove

1 small red onion

2 small (Persian) cucumbers

1 green pepper

1 Serrano chilli (red or green)

60 ml extra virgin olive oil

60 ml Jerez sherry vinegar

sea salt flakes and cracked black pepper

fruity olive oil, to drizzle

chives, to garnish (optional)

SMOKED SALTED TOASTS

1 small baguette

1 garlic clove, finely chopped

60 ml olive oil

1 tablespoon smoked sea salt

SERVES 4

Try making this refreshing summer soup with heirloom tomatoes of different colours. If you can't find them, use any very ripe and tasty tomatoes. The sherry vinegar is the key to gazpacho, so seek out a heady one from Jerez in Spain — it will make all the difference.

To peel the tomatoes, fill a small bowl with ice and water and set aside. Bring a medium-sized saucepan of water to the boil. Using a sharp knife, score a cross in the top of each tomato. Drop the tomatoes into the hot water for just 30 seconds. Remove with a slotted spoon and drop into the iced water for 1 minute. Remove from the water and peel. Cut the tomatoes in halves or quarters, depending on the size, and put in the food processor.

Roughly chop the garlic, onion and cucumbers then add to the tomatoes. Cut the green pepper and Serrano chilli in half and remove the white pith and seeds. Chop both and add to the tomatoes. Pulse the mixture until it is chunky. Pour the gazpacho into a large bowl and stir in the olive oil and vinegar. Chill in the refrigerator until ready to serve.

Preheat the oven to 200°C (400°F) Gas 6.

To make the Smoked Salted Toasts, slice the baguette lengthways into 4 and lay the slices on a baking tray. Mix the garlic and olive oil in a small bowl and drizzle over the bread. Sprinkle with the smoked sea salt and bake in the preheated oven for 8–10 minutes until golden.

Pour the gazpacho into 4 bowls, season with the sea salt flakes and cracked black pepper, drizzle each bowl with a little olive oil and garnish with a few chives, if liked. Serve each bowl with a Smoked Salted Toast on the side.

chickpea, tomato and green bean minestrone

2 tablespoons olive oil

1 onion, chopped

2 garlic cloves, chopped

400-g tin chickpeas, rinsed and drained

100 g green beans, sliced on the angle

6 ripe tomatoes, halved

1 handful of chopped fresh flat leaf parsley

1.5 litres vegetable stock

100 g spaghetti, broken into short lengths

50 g wild rocket leaves

50 g Pecorino or Parmesan, finely grated

sea salt and freshly ground black pepper

crusty bread, to serve

SERVES 4

Minestrone can be a hotchpotch of whatever takes your fancy. Often thought of as cold weather fare, this version has summer written all over it and is packed with fresh tomatoes and green beans as well as chickpeas, a store-cupboard staple you should never be without. A few handfuls of fresh rocket make a nice addition, as its peppery bite and fresh taste lightens the soup making it an ideal starter.

Put the oil in a large saucepan set over medium heat. Add the onion, partially cover with a lid and cook for 4–5 minutes, stirring often, until softened. Add the garlic and cook for 1 minute. Add the chickpeas, green beans, tomatoes, parsley, stock and spaghetti and bring to the boil.

Reduce the heat and let simmer, uncovered, for about 15–20 minutes, stirring often, until the spaghetti is cooked and the soup has thickened. Season to taste with salt and pepper.

Just before serving, add the rocket and gently stir until the rocket wilts and softens. Ladle into warmed serving bowls and sprinkle a generous amount of grated cheese over the top. Serve immediately with chunks of crusty bread on the side.

crab bisque

600 g cooked whole crab

1.2 litres fish stock

150 ml white wine

50 g unsalted butter

3 leeks, sliced

300 g potatoes, peeled
and diced

1 teaspoon tomato purée

3 tablespoons brandy

2 fresh tarragon sprigs

3 tablespoons double cream

¼ teaspoon ground mace

freshly squeezed juice of
½ a lemon

sea salt

a pinch of cayenne pepper,
to serve

crusty bread, to serve

SERVES 4

This impressive soup is very easy to make and is reminiscent of those rust-hued Mediterranean soups which taste of shellfish and have a hint of chilli in them. For convenience, buy fresh, prepared crabmeat which comes in its shell.

Prise out the white and brown crabmeat from its shell, place in a small bowl and reserve. You should have at least 250 g meat. Put the shell, stock and wine in a saucepan and simmer for 20 minutes.

Heat the butter in a large frying pan set over low heat, then add the leeks. Cover and cook for 5 minutes until softened, but not browned. Add the potatoes and stir well, then replace the lid and cook for a further 5 minutes, stirring occasionally to stop it from sticking. Add the tomato purée, brandy and tarragon and turn up the heat to burn off the alcohol. Once it has evaporated, strain in half the stock mixture and simmer until the potatoes are completely soft, about 15 minutes.

Transfer the contents of the frying pan to a blender and liquidize until smooth. Return to the pan, strain in the remaining stock, then add the reserved crabmeat and the cream. Heat through and season to taste with salt, mace and lemon juice.

Divide the soup between 4 serving bowls, sprinkle with a little cayenne pepper and serve with crusty bread on the side.

salads

double courgette, parmesan and walnut salad

3 tablespoons freshly squeezed lemon juice

finely grated zest of 2 lemons

½ teaspoon sea salt

6 tablespoons extra virgin olive oil

12 small (baby) courgettes

6 medium courgettes

70 g walnuts, toasted

leaves from a small bunch of fresh basil or mint, chopped

50 g fresh Parmesan, shaved

freshly ground black pepper

a ridged grill pan

SERVES 6

This unusual and tasty salad is a combination of two styles of courgette; larger ones marinated and grilled for a deep flavour and soft texture, and baby courgettes very thinly sliced and marinated for a crunchy texture and fresh flavour.

To make the marinade, whisk together the lemon juice and zest with the salt and ¼ teaspoon black pepper in a small bowl, then slowly whisk in the oil.

Slice the small courgettes as thinly as possible, using a mandoline if you have one. Put in a shallow, non-reactive dish and pour over half the marinade. Cover and leave to marinate at room temperature for at least 1 hour and up to 6 hours, turning occasionally.

Thickly slice the medium courgettes and put them in another shallow, non-reactive dish. Pour over the remaining marinade, cover and leave to marinate at room temperature for 1 hour.

Heat a ridged grill pan until hot and pan-grill the medium courgettes for 1–2 minutes on each side. Let cool. Arrange both the marinated and grilled courgettes together on a serving dish and scatter over the walnuts and basil. Finish with shavings of Parmesan and freshly ground black pepper.

apple, beetroot and fennel salad with roquefort

1 bunch of watercress, stems trimmed, leaves rinsed and dried

2 crisp green eating apples, halved, cored, and thinly sliced

1 fennel bulb, halved and thinly sliced

75 g Roquefort cheese, crumbled

a handful of fresh flat leaf parsley, finely chopped

a small bunch of chives, snipped

2 cooked beetroots

FOR THE VINAIGRETTE

2 tablespoons red or white wine vinegar

1 teaspoon fine sea salt

1 teaspoon Dijon mustard

7 tablespoons sunflower oil

1 tablespoon crème fraîche or soured cream

freshly ground black pepper

SERVES 4

This is a colourful combination of crisp ingredients that makes a lively start to any meal. The mix of flavours and textures is very pleasing; if fennel is unavailable, you could substitute two celery stalks, thinly sliced.

First, prepare the vinaigrette. Put the vinegar in a bowl. Using a fork or a small whisk, stir in the salt until almost dissolved. Stir in the mustard. Stir in the oil, a tablespoon at a time, whisking well between each addition, until emulsified. Finally, stir in the crème fraîche and add pepper to taste.

Just before you're ready to serve the salad, tear the watercress into pieces and put it in a bowl with the apples, fennel, cheese, parsley and chives. Pour over all but 2 tablespoons of the vinaigrette and toss gently with your hands.

Divide the salad between 4 serving plates and top each portion with some slices of beetroot. Drizzle the remaining vinaigrette over the top of each salad and serve immediately.

classic caesar salad

This recipe is a rare perfection as it's true to the original classic Caesar salad. It makes a perfect starter as it's light but full of flavour. To make a more substantial meal, just follow any of the additions listed below.

2 thick slices of dense white bread

2 tablespoons olive oil

1 large or 3 baby cos lettuce

40 g fresh Parmesan, grated or shaved

CLASSIC CAESAR DRESSING

1 very fresh egg*, at room temperature

1 small garlic clove, crushed

1 teaspoon Dijon mustard

1 teaspoon Worcestershire sauce

¼ teaspoon sea salt

⅛ teaspoon freshly ground black pepper

1 tablespoon white wine vinegar

1 tablespoon freshly squeezed lemon juice

4 tablespoons extra virgin olive oil

4 anchovy fillets, finely chopped (optional)

SERVES 4

Cut the crusts off the bread and discard. Cut the bread into cubes. Heat the olive oil in a frying pan, add the bread cubes and cook until golden brown. Set aside.

To make the Classic Caesar Dressing, put the egg in a small saucepan and cover with warm water. Bring to just simmering, turn off the heat and leave for 2 minutes. Run under cold water to stop the egg cooking any further.

Crack the egg into a large serving bowl and whisk in the garlic, mustard, Worcestershire sauce, salt, pepper, vinegar and lemon juice. Slowly whisk in the extra virgin olive oil. Stir in the chopped anchovy fillets, if using. Add the lettuce to the bowl and toss well. Transfer to 4 serving plates then scatter over the Parmesan cheese and croûtons to serve.

Variations:

Chicken Caesar Roast 3–4 chicken breasts, preferably in a roasting bag to prevent them drying out, until golden and cooked through. Let cool then slice and add to the salad.

Bacon and avocado Caesar Fry 8 rashers of bacon until crisp. Chop and add to the salad with 1 sliced avocado.

*Note This recipe uses partially cooked eggs. If you prefer to cook the eggs through, you can do this by increasing the cooking time to 6 minutes. Finely chop the egg before adding it to the dressing.

cherry tomato, bocconcini and basil salad on bruschetta

4 tablespoons extra virgin olive oil

1 teaspoon balsamic vinegar

12 bocconcini, halved, or 375 g regular mozzarella cheese, cubed

20 ripe cherry tomatoes or pomodorini (baby plum tomatoes), halved

a handful of torn fresh basil leaves, plus extra to serve

125 g wild rocket leaves

sea salt and freshly ground black pepper

FOR THE BRUSCHETTA

4 thick slices country bread, preferably sourdough

2 garlic cloves, halved

extra virgin olive oil, for drizzling

SERVES 4

All the colours of the Italian flag are here in this delicious salad. This makes a great start to a rustic summer meal and the bruschetta is optional if you want an even lighter bite. *Bocconcini* (meaning 'little bites') are tiny balls of mozzarella – they are the perfect size for this recipe but if you can't find them, use regular mozzarella cut into cubes.

Whisk 3 tablespoons of the olive oil with the balsamic vinegar. Season to taste with salt and pepper. Stir in the halved bocconcini or mozzarella cubes, tomatoes and torn basil leaves. Set aside.

To make the bruschetta, grill, toast or pan-grill the bread on both sides until lightly charred or toasted. Rub the top side of each slice with the cut garlic, then drizzle with olive oil.

Cover each slice of bruschetta with rocket and spoon over the tomatoes and mozzarella. Drizzle with the remaining olive oil and top with fresh basil leaves. Serve immediately as the bread will quickly become soggy.

meat and poultry

parma ham with figs and balsamic dressing

4 large fresh ripe figs (preferably purple ones)

1 tablespoon good balsamic vinegar

extra virgin olive oil, to drizzle

12 thin slices of Parma ham or prosciutto crudo

150 g fresh Parmesan, broken into rough chunks

extra virgin olive oil, to serve

cracked black pepper

SERVES 4

This is an all-time classic recipe. The combination of sweet, salty Parma ham and a soft, yielding ripe fig is one of life's little miracles. Choose a very good quality aged balsamic vinegar – it should be thick, sweet and syrupy – and use it in tiny amounts. This is quick and easy to assemble, and best served at room temperature, rather than chilled, for maximum flavour.

Take each fig and stand it upright. Using a sharp knife, make 2 cuts across each fig not quite quartering it, but keeping it intact. Ease the figs open to form a 'flower' and brush with balsamic vinegar and olive oil.

Arrange 3 slices of Parma ham on each of 4 serving plates. Place a fig on top and scatter the Parmesan chunks over and around the fig. Drizzle with extra virgin olive oil and sprinkle with plenty of cracked black pepper. Serve at room temperature rather than chilled for maximum flavour.

chicken liver pâté
with blueberry and balsamic glaze

2 tablespoons olive oil

1 onion, finely chopped

2 garlic cloves, chopped

2 bay leaves

500 g chicken livers, cleaned and trimmed*

1 tablespoon ruby port

2 teaspoons soy sauce

¼ teaspoon ground nutmeg

¼ teaspoon ground cinnamon

½ teaspoon sea salt

¼ teaspoon freshly ground black pepper

fresh thyme, to garnish (optional)

grissini (Italian bread sticks), to serve

BLUEBERRY AND BALSAMIC GLAZE

200 g fresh or frozen blueberries

60 g sugar

2 sheets of leaf gelatine

1 tablespoon balsamic vinegar

6 ramekins or small glass dishes

SERVES 6

This is a less rich, dairy-free alternative to traditional chicken liver pâté with a fruity glaze. It's a good choice as a starter as it's not too filling, especially when served with *grissini* instead of the more usual buttered toast.

To make the blueberry and balsamic glaze, put the blueberries, sugar and 75 ml water in a saucepan. Bring to the boil, then continue to cook for 3 minutes. Strain through a fine sieve to give about 150 ml liquid. Soak the leaf gelatine in cold water for a few minutes to soften then squeeze out any excess water and add the leaves to the hot blueberry mixture, along with the balsamic vinegar. Stir to dissolve. Leave to cool slightly before using.

Heat the olive oil in a large frying pan set over medium heat. Add the onion, garlic and bay leaves and sauté for 5 minutes, until the onion is translucent. Increase the heat, add the chicken livers and cook them, stirring, for 2–3 minutes until firm but still pink in the middle. Remove from the heat and discard the bay leaves. Spoon the chicken liver mixture into a food processor and add the port, soy sauce, nutmeg, cinnamon, salt and pepper. Process in short bursts until you have a smooth pâté.

Spoon the pâté into 6 ramekins, level the tops and pour the blueberry glaze over the top. Leave to set then garnish with thyme, if using, and serve with grissini. This pâté will keep in the refrigerator for up to 3 days.

*Note To clean chicken livers, cut off any green specks of bile, pull away any sinew and connective tissue and discard, then rinse the livers.

seared steak carpaccio
with truffle vinaigrette and rocket

500 g fillet steak*

2 tablespoons mixed peppercorns

1 teaspoon herbes de Provence

2 tablespoons olive oil

100 g wild rocket leaves

TRUFFLE VINAIGRETTE

2 tablespoons white wine vinegar

½ teaspoon balsamic vinegar

2 teaspoons white truffle-flavoured olive oil

6 tablespoons light olive oil

2 tablespoons whipping cream

sea salt and freshly ground black pepper

shavings of fresh Parmesan, to serve

crusty bread, to serve (optional)

SERVES 6

Carpaccio is traditionally a raw steak dish, but in this version the meat is well seasoned and seared first. It makes an easy yet fabulously showy and colourful dinner party starter.

Trim the beef of any excess fat or sinew and pat dry with kitchen paper. Put the peppercorns in a mortar with the herbes de Provence and pound with a pestle until crushed. Coat all sides of the meat with the crushed peppercorns, wrap in clingfilm and chill in the refrigerator for 1 hour.

Heat a frying pan over medium to high heat for about 3 minutes until hot. Add the oil, heat for 1 minute, then brown the meat on all sides for 2–3 minutes, turning regularly to prevent the peppercorns burning. Set aside to cool, then rewrap the meat and put it in the freezer for about 45 minutes until firm.

To make the vinaigrette, put the vinegars in a bowl and season with salt and pepper. Whisk in the oils until the dressing is thick, then gradually add the cream. Taste and adjust the seasoning and set aside.

Slice the beef as thinly as you can with a very sharp knife and lay it between sheets of greaseproof paper. Beat it out with a meat mallet or rolling pin to make it thinner still.

Arrange the rocket leaves on each of 4 serving plates, then lay over the slices of carpaccio. Spoon a little dressing over each portion. Top with shavings of Parmesan and serve with crusty bread, if liked.

*Note It's important to buy a piece of meat of an even thickness so that it cooks evenly.

pork and hazelnut rillettes

with pickled cucumbers

1 kg pork belly, derinded

7 fresh thyme sprigs

2 large garlic cloves, peeled

1 bay leaf

1 teaspoon sea salt

½ teaspoon freshly ground
black pepper

125 ml white wine

75 g whole blanched hazelnuts

toasted bread, to serve

PICKLED CUCUMBERS

15-cm length of cucumber

125 ml rice vinegar

125 g sugar

*6 individual serving pots or
ramekins, each 125 ml capacity*

SERVES 6

A traditional means of preserving meat in fat, rillettes are a deliciously simple alternative to a heartier terrine. The hazelnuts add a lovely flavour as well as a delicious crunch and the tartness of the pickled cucumbers is just right.

To make the pickled cucumbers, cut the cucumber in half lengthways and scoop out the seeds. Cut the flesh into very thin strips.

Put the rice vinegar and sugar in a saucepan and bring to the boil, stirring until the sugar has dissolved. Boil for 3 minutes. Cool and pour over the cucumber. Cover and refrigerate until needed.

Cut the pork belly into small pieces and put in a small, heavy-based casserole. Add 1 thyme sprig (reserving the rest as a garnish), the garlic, bay leaf, salt and pepper and pour over the wine. Cover and cook over low heat for 3 hours until the meat is very tender.

Preheat the oven to 160°C (325°F) Gas 3.

Spread out the hazelnuts in an even layer on a baking tray. Bake in the preheated oven for 20 minutes, stirring occasionally, until the nuts are just smelling toasted. Put them in a clean tea towel and rub vigorously until the skins come loose. Discard the skins and roughly chop the nuts.

Transfer the pork into a colander set over a large bowl or jug, reserving all the juices. Using 2 forks, tear the pork into fine strips, or process briefly in a food processor. Combine the meat with the toasted hazelnuts and pack into the pots. Spoon the fatty juices over the meat and finish with a thyme sprig to garnish. Once cool, keep refrigerated until ready to serve. These rillettes will keep in refrigerator for up to 3 days.

fish and seafood

salt-crusted citrus prawns
with chilli dipping sauce

finely grated zest and freshly
squeezed juice of 2 limes

1.8 kg coarse sea salt

450 g large raw prawns such
as tiger prawns, unshelled

CHILLI DIPPING SAUCE

2 red chillies, finely chopped

4 fresh kaffir lime leaves,
finely shredded

1 spring onion, finely chopped

1 garlic clove, finely chopped

125 ml fish sauce

finely grated zest and freshly
squeezed juice of 2 limes

1 tablespoon rice wine vinegar

1 tablespoon brown sugar

1 tablespoon unsalted peanuts,
chopped

SERVES 4

This is a showstopper at any dinner party. Crack open the salt crust at the table and let your guests be dazzled by the heavenly aromas and the bright pink shells.

Preheat the oven to 240°C (475°F) Gas 9.

In a large bowl mix together the lime zest and juice, salt and 250 ml water. The mixture should be the consistency of wet sand. Spread a layer of the salt mixture in a baking dish and arrange the prawns on top. Cover with the remaining salt mixture and pat well down, making sure the prawns are completely covered and there are no gaps anywhere.

Bake in the preheated oven for 15 minutes. The salt should be slightly golden on top.

Whisk together all the Chilli Dipping Sauce ingredients until the sugar has dissolved. Divide between 4 small bowls.

When the prawns are ready, take them out of the oven and leave them to rest for 5 minutes. Using the back of a knife, crack open the crust and remove the top part. Serve at the table.

Let guests help themselves, peel their own prawns, and dip in the chilli sauce. Have a large empty bowl handy for the shells.

smoked mackerel and preserved lemon pâté
with harissa crushed tomatoes

250 g smoked mackerel fillets, skinned

rind of 1 small preserved lemon*, finely chopped

3 tablespoons finely chopped fresh dill

250 g cream cheese, softened

crisply toasted flat breads, to serve

HARISSA CRUSHED TOMATOES

300 g cherry tomatoes

1 tablespoon harissa (spicy Moroccan chilli paste)

6–8 ramekins

SERVES 8

A wonderfully quick pâté using smoked mackerel or any other moist smoked fish, this makes a simple yet impressive and delicious start to a dinner party.

Remove the skin and any stray bones from the mackerel fillets, flake the flesh into a bowl and mix with the preserved lemon, dill and cream cheese. Cover and refrigerate until ready to serve.

In a small serving bowl, combine the cherry tomatoes and harissa, crushing the tomatoes lightly with the back of a fork.

Divide the pâté between the ramekins and serve with the Harissa Crushed Tomatoes and crisply toasted flat breads.

*Note Preserved lemons are used extensively in North African cooking and are whole lemons packed in jars with salt. The interesting thing is that you eat only the rind, which contains the essential flavour of the lemon. They are available from larger supermarkets and specialist online retailers.

pickled salmon with fennel and cucumber salad

500-g salmon fillet, skinned and boned

3–4 shallots, thinly sliced

4 tablespoons chopped dill

1 fennel bulb, with fronds if possible

½ cucumber, halved lengthways and deseeded

freshly squeezed juice of 1 lemon

1 teaspoon wholegrain mustard

3 tablespoons olive oil, plus extra for drizzling

sea salt and freshly ground black pepper

PICKLING LIQUID

200 ml white or rice vinegar

2 teaspoons sea salt

4 tablespoons sugar

finely grated zest of 1 lemon

SERVES 4

This is a light and refreshing starter. The fish is marinated for several days, so do prepare ahead. Serve with boiled and buttered new potatoes to make a more substantial meal.

To make the pickling liquid, combine the vinegar, 100 ml water, salt, sugar and lemon zest in a saucepan and bring to the boil. Simmer for 3 minutes, then let cool.

Put the salmon fillet in a shallow, non-reactive container with the shallots and dill. Pour over the pickling liquid and cover tightly. Leave in the refrigerator for 2–3 days, turning the salmon once a day.

To assemble the salad, remove the salmon from the pickling liquid and slice it into thin strips. Arrange the salmon on 4 serving plates with a few of the pickled shallots.

Slice the fennel and cucumber very thinly, using a mandoline if you have one, and put in a bowl. Chop the green fennel fronds, if available, very finely and add 3 tablespoonfuls to the bowl.

In a small bowl, whisk together the lemon juice, mustard and oil and season to taste with salt and pepper. Just before serving, toss the dressing through the fennel and cucumber salad and arrange a little on top of the salmon. Drizzle with extra oil to serve.

chilli salt squid

400 g cleaned squid
(1 large tube)

2 tablespoons cornflour

1 tablespoon plain flour

½ teaspoon ground white pepper

½ teaspoon mild chilli powder

3 teaspoons sea salt

1 large red chilli, thinly sliced

a small handful of fresh coriander
leaves, chopped

vegetable oil, for deep-frying

lemon or lime wedges, to serve

SERVES 4

This is a delicious starter that's perfect for sharing when served on a single platter. Fresh squid can seem a little scary, but it really is superior to frozen. Serve it with plenty of lemon or lime wedges for squeezing and a nice thirst-quenching aperitif to counter the chilli.

Cut the squid tube down one side so that it opens up. Use a sharp knife to trim and discard any internal membranes. Cut it lengthways into 2-cm wide strips, then cut each strip in half. Combine the cornflour, flour, pepper, chilli powder and salt in a large bowl. Half-fill a large saucepan with the vegetable oil and heat over high heat until the surface of the oil shimmers.

Toss half of the squid pieces in the flour mixture, quickly shaking off the excess, and add them to the oil. Cook for about 2 minutes, until deep golden. Remove with a slotted spoon and drain on kitchen paper. Repeat with the remaining squid. Add the chilli slices to the oil and cook for just a few seconds.

Remove from the pan and drain on kitchen paper. Put the squid and chilli on a serving platter and sprinkle with the coriander. Serve while still warm with plenty of lemon wedges on the side for squeezing.

vegetarian

smoked mushroom pâté

150 g cream cheese
½ teaspoon sea salt
6 tablespoons fresh dill
75 g butter
crackers or toast, to serve

SMOKED MUSHROOMS
70 g plain flour
115 g sugar
115 g rice
30 g tea leaves
350 g fresh flat mushrooms
125 ml olive oil

an aluminium foil roasting dish
or wok
a large ramekin

SERVE 4–6

This delicious recipe showcases the wonderful flavours of the smoked mushrooms. If you can find pre-smoked mushrooms, by all means use them – you will need 300 g. Otherwise, it is quite easy to smoke your own at home.

Preheat a barbecue or element.

To make the smoked mushrooms, mix together the flour, sugar, rice and tea and spread over the bottom of the roasting dish or wok.

Put the mushrooms in a single layer on a metal rack. Place the rack on the roasting dish containing the tea-leaf mixture. Cover loosely with a large piece of aluminium foil and crimp the edges to the roasting dish securely so that no smoke escapes.

Place on the preheated barbecue or element and heat for 15 minutes. Remove from the heat and leave, covered, to cool. Put the cooled mushrooms in a container and cover with the olive oil. Refrigerate until needed.

Put the drained smoked mushrooms, cream cheese and salt in a food processor and process in bursts until well combined. Add 4 tablespoons of the dill and fold through. Spoon the pâté into the ramekin and smooth over the top. Chop the remaining dill and scatter over the pâté.

Melt the butter in a small saucepan. Remove from the heat and let the milk solids settle at the bottom, then pour the clarified butter over the top of the pâté, taking care to pour in as few of the milk solids as possible. Serve with crackers or toast.

cheese and basil souffles

200 ml whole milk

4–6 sprigs of fresh basil

4 large eggs (or 5 if your whites
are unusually small)

25 g butter

20 g plain flour

50 g mature Gruyère or Cheddar,
grated

25 g Parmesan, freshly grated,
plus extra to dust the soufflé dish

sea salt and freshly ground
black pepper

*a 15-cm soufflé dish, about 9 cm
high, or 4 individual ramekins,
lightly buttered*

SERVES 4

Soufflés are one of the most impressive dishes you can
make for your guests. You can make this delicious version
in individual ramekins, as shown here, if you prefer. Simply
reduce the baking time to 20–25 minutes.

Put the milk in a saucepan, add the basil and bring slowly to the boil.
Turn the heat very low, simmer for 1 minute, then turn off the heat and
leave the basil to infuse for about 20 minutes.

Meanwhile, separate the eggs carefully — put the whites in a large, clean
grease-free bowl and set aside 3 of the yolks to add to the sauce.

Preheat the oven to 200°C (400°F) Gas 6.

Set a large, heavy-based saucepan over medium heat and add the butter.
When melted, stir in the flour. Cook for a few seconds, then pour in the
warm, basil-infused milk through a sieve. Whisk together until smooth,
then cook over low heat until thick. Stir in the grated Gruyère and most
of the Parmesan and set back over low heat until the cheese has melted.
Leave to cool for 5 minutes. Stir in the 3 egg yolks one by one.

Sprinkle the inside of the buttered soufflé dish with a little Parmesan,
shaking off any excess. Put the dish on a baking tray.

Whisk the egg whites and a pinch of salt until holding their shape but
not stiff. Take 2 tablespoons of the whites and fold into the cheese base,
then carefully fold in the rest of the whites without overmixing. Tip
the mixture into the prepared soufflé dish. Sprinkle with a little more
Parmesan and bake in the preheated oven for 25–30 minutes until the
soufflé is well risen and browned. (Don't open the oven door or your
soufflé may collapse!) Serve immediately.

naked spinach and ricotta ravioli
with sage cream

1 kg fresh spinach, well washed and roughly chopped

250 g ricotta

5 egg yolks

125 g Parmesan, finely grated, plus extra to serve

125 g plain flour

1 tablespoon butter

12 fresh sage leaves

250 ml single cream

sea salt and freshly ground black pepper

a baking tray lined with baking paper

SERVES 3-4

These little balls of spinach and ricotta are called 'naked' ravioli, as they are missing the pasta wrapping that usually encloses the filling. They can be made a day in advance and chilled in the fridge until you are ready to cook them.

Bring a large saucepan of water to the boil. Add the spinach and cook for 5 minutes, until wilted and tender. Rinse with cold water and drain well.

Tip the cooked spinach into the centre of a clean tea towel. (This process will stain the tea towel so use an old, threadbare one, rather than your best.) Roll the tea towel up to form a log and twist the ends away from each other to squeeze out as much liquid as possible. Put the spinach on a chopping board and chop finely. Transfer to a large bowl. Add the ricotta, egg yolks and half of the Parmesan and season to taste with salt and pepper. Mix well to thoroughly combine.

Put the flour on a large plate. Using slightly wet hands, roll the spinach mixture into 12 walnut-sized balls. Lightly roll each ball in the flour and put them on the prepared baking tray.

Put the butter and sage in a small saucepan and set over medium heat. Cook until the sage leaves just sizzle. Add the cream and the remaining Parmesan and cook for about 10 minutes, until thickened, stirring often to prevent the cream from catching on the bottom of the pan.

Bring a large saucepan of lightly salted water to the boil. Carefully drop the balls into the boiling water and cook for just 1 minute, until they rise to the surface. Drain well and arrange 3 or 4 balls in each serving dish. Spoon over the warm sage cream, sprinkle with the extra Parmesan and grind over plenty of black pepper. Serve immediately.

fresh asparagus
with home-made hollandaise sauce

500 g fresh asparagus spears, trimmed
cracked black pepper

HOLLANDAISE SAUCE
150 g unsalted butter
2 tablespoons white wine vinegar
1 shallot, finely chopped
a pinch of sea salt
2 egg yolks

SERVES 4

Hollandaise is a smooth emulsion of butter, vinegar and eggs. Rich and velvety, this sauce is pure heaven when partnered with simply cooked asparagus, and makes an indulgent yet light start to any elegant meal.

To make the hollandaise, melt the butter very gently in a small saucepan. Pour it into a small jug through a muslin-lined tea strainer to remove any excess milk solids.

Put the vinegar, shallot, salt and 1 tablespoon water in a small saucepan and heat gently until the liquid is almost totally evaporated, leaving only about 1 tablespoon. Remove from the heat and strain into a glass bowl.

Place the bowl over a saucepan of gently simmering water (do not let the bowl touch the water). Add the egg yolks and, using a balloon whisk, whisk the mixture for 2 minutes, or until pale and frothy. Remove from the heat.

Using an electric whisk, whisk in the melted butter, pouring it in in a slow, steady stream. Continue whisking until the sauce becomes thick and velvety. Cover and keep warm.

Steam or boil the asparagus, as preferred and arrange on 4 serving plates. Spoon over the warm hollandaise, sprinkle with a little cracked black pepper and serve immediately.

index